Little Pebble™

Construction Vehicles at Work

Excavators

by Kathryn Clay

CAPSTONE PRESS
a capstone imprint

Little Pebble is published by Capstone Press,
1710 Roe Crest Drive, North Mankato, Minnesota 56003
www.mycapstone.com

Library of Congress Cataloging-in-Publication Data
Cataloging-in-publication information is on file with the Library of Congress.
ISBN 978-1-5157-8015-1 (library binding)
ISBN 978-1-5157-8017-5 (paperback)
ISBN 978-1-5157-8019-9 (eBook PDF)
Written by Kathryn Clay.

Editorial Credits
Shelly Lyons, editor; Juliette Peters, designer;
Wanda Winch, media researcher; Laura Manthe, production specialist

Photo Credits
Alamy: Dan Leeth, 13; Shutterstock: a2i, cover, CBCK, 17, Guenter Albers, 9, Janos Huszka, metal plate and stripe design, Maria Jeffs, 15, Milos Stojanovic, 21, mosher, 11, Natykach Nataliia, 3, Nicolae Cucurudza, 5, Pablos33, concrete texture, Tsuguliev, 1, Vadim Ratnikov, 7, 19, Volodymyr Hlukhovskyi, dirt texture, Yuliyan Velchev, metal texture

Printed in China.
010290F17

Table of Contents

About Excavators

Look!

This is an excavator.

It is also called a digger.

Diggers have tracks.

The tracks turn.

tracks

See the boom?

It moves the arm.

boom

arm

Here is the bucket.

It is like a spoon.

It dips. It picks up dirt.

bucket

At Work

Jen sits in the cab.

She runs the digger.

cab

Diggers lift rocks.

They move dirt.

The digger makes
a hole.
A house will be built.

A digger makes
the land smooth.
A road is put down.

We fix a pipe.

A digger helps.

Thanks, digger!

Glossary

arm—the long metal piece that holds the bucket

boom—the long metal piece that moves the arm

bucket—the scoop

cab—the place where the driver sits

track—a metal belt that runs around wheels

Read More

Carr, Aaron. *Excavators.* Mighty Machines.
New York: Weigl, 2013.

Lennie, Charles. *Excavators.* Construction Machines.
Minneapolis: Abdo Kids, 2015.

Pallotta, Jerry. *The Construction Alphabet Book.*
Watertown, Mass.: Charlesbridge, 2017.

Internet Sites

FactHound offers a safe, fun way to find Internet sites
related to this book. All of the sites on FactHound
have been researched by our staff.

Here's all you do:
Visit *www.facthound.com*
Type in this code: 9781515780151

Check out projects, games and lots more at
www.capstonekids.com

Index